Jn 14.16 ESV

The Helper

Journey into Purposeful Work

Andy Black

Onwards and Upwards Publishers

Berkeley House, 11 Nightingale Crescent,
Leatherhead, Surrey, KT24 6PD.
www.onwardsandupwards.org

Printed in the UK.

ISBN: 978-1-911086-03-1
Typeface: Sabon LT
Graphic design: LM Graphic Design

The author would like to express his indebtedness to Albert Camus, the French philosopher, for his excellent symbolism of Sisyphus in connection with the futility of work in modern times.

Endorsements

We live in times when the desire to do something worthwhile and personally satisfying with our lives has never been greater. This easily accessible but highly practical book is a great guide for anyone seeking purpose and impact. Drawing on his own journey the author guides the reader with precision and understanding towards that future. Titled 'The Helper', just like the Holy Spirit, he comes alongside to help, to draw out of you what was already inside.

"The plans of a man are like deep water and a man of wisdom draws them out." (Proverbs 20:5)

Paul Manwaring
Senior leadership team, Bethel church, Redding, California
Director, Global Legacy
Author of 'Kisses from a Good God' and 'What on Earth is Glory'. Destiny Publishing.
paulmanwaring.com.

'The Helper' is an honest and vulnerable 'fly on the wall' view into the working, spiritual and emotional life of Andy Black.

His story is compelling, challenging and insightful. I found myself identifying with many of his experiences in the workplace and his journey with God.

It's a story of hope, perseverance and most of all faith.

Whatever your work life looks like, 'The Helper' will inspire and encourage you to be all that you can be and to follow your dreams.

Sue Eldridge
Senior Leader, Presence Church
Director of Presence Ministries International
North Yorkshire, England

3

The Helper

We are living in the days of kingdom expansion. Part of this understanding is the challenge to bring kingdom culture and kingdom solutions to all spheres of society. This includes the workplace. As such, believers are being challenged to embark upon a journey to perform their work as a calling; not just as a place to earn money, but to be fruitful in every respect.

In his book 'The Helper' Andy Black describes such a journey.

Here is a powerful encouragement to pursue, with God's help, the dreams of your heart even if they have not yet become completely clear. Andy's personal story kindles the hope that following these dreams will actually propel us into our destiny so that our life becomes truly meaningful and will have the impact that it was originally designed to have.

It is even more encouraging to read how God will meet you in the middle of your pursuit and make it absolutely evident that he is interested in you living a fulfilled life. What a blessing!

Martin Spreer
Senior Pastor, Christ-Church, Duisburg, Germany

There are very few people who don't, at some point in their lives, question whether they're in the wrong line of work. Andy's very readable book provides some vital advice on how to navigate the sometimes frightening terrain between frustration and fulfilment. Using stories from his own journey, he provides a map of how, with God's help, we can travel with faith to a point where passion and profession converge, giving us a reason not only to wake up in the morning, but to get up too.

Mark Stibbe
Bestselling author
CEO of Kingdom Writing Solutions

This is a different decade for Christians and the world of work. A decade in which the church has woken up to its privilege and responsibility to equip members to serve God in their workplace settings. A decade too in which, thankfully, scores of helpful and equipping books have been written.

This book, 'The Helper', stands out. The authentic vulnerable narrative takes us into a world where many years in the wrong job left Andy Black and his wife with searching, penetrating and disturbing questions about their world of work.

With no quick solutions and no easy answers, Andy then takes his readers into a breakthrough moment with God which transformed his life and his work. This book will inspire all, but may well hold the keys for many who are struggling with a job they currently feel trapped in. I heartily recommend this read.

David Oliver
Salt & Light Ministries
Author of 'Work – Prison or Place of Destiny?' and
'Love Work Live Life'

Acknowledgements

To Adrienne
My best friend, now and always

I would also like to thank:

My family editorial team of Adrienne, Hannah, Darren, Caroline,
James and Becky for giving your precious time to dedicated scrutiny
of the draft material leading to some very valuable feedback.
I love you all more than words can say.

Tim Eldridge, my church leader, for affirming my calling.
I am immensely grateful to God for this spiritual heart
knitting over the years.

Luke Jeffery and the Onwards and Upwards Publishers team for
gently introducing me into the hitherto unknown world of
publishing; then transforming my efforts into a presentation with
the potential to impact many lives in a positive way.

Contents

The Helper

Foreword by Tim Eldridge

ANDY'S BOOK REVEALS A GREAT TRUTH. Work was never intended to be a place where we simply earn a living, but rather one where we accomplish something of worth. God has put creativity in each one of us because we carry his DNA. This is expressed in so many different ways, each with a unique outworking.

I believe this is available for everyone, but it is the follower of Christ who begins to understand this truth more fully through God's Word, such as:

> For we are God's workmanship, created in Christ Jesus to do good works, which God prepared in advance for us to do.
>
> Ephesians 2:10 (NIV)

For most people, work fills our lives for forty hours each week for forty years, so to experience exciting opportunities through all that time is surely preferred to the drudgery that often occurs. As we seek after God rather than 'things' like money, careers or position, he blesses us and reveals the next steps in his purposes.

I have known Andy for over twenty years and been his pastor for seventeen of those. I have observed a significant part of his journey, his searching and discovery of his workplace ministry. It has been a pleasure to watch how he has found what God had hidden for him to do. His breakthrough has now led to many others breaking through too. He has taught me many aspects of what it means to steward God's presence in the place of work. Enjoy this book and be ready to be challenged.

Tim Eldridge
Senior Leader, Presence Church
Director of Presence Ministries International
North Yorkshire, England.

Prologue

IN GREEK LEGEND, THE GODS devise an eternal punishment for a man named Sisyphus: to push a rock up a mountain. Each time he reaches the top, the rock rolls back down and he has to start all over again from the bottom. It is a meaningless task.

The certainty of Sisyphus' fate enabled him to recognise the absurdity of his plight and to carry on with contented acceptance.

> The workman of today works every day in his life at the same tasks, and this fate is no less absurd [than Sisyphus'] and is tragic only at rare moments when it becomes conscious.[1]

I once knew a retired man who had a story to tell of a futile working life. He worked for forty years in the aerospace industry only to see all his efforts dumped in a skip on the day he was made redundant. It made him feel sick to think of all his wasted effort. If only he'd known at the beginning how to work for something that would have a lasting purpose.

My story is different. God intervened.

As a young man straight out of school, I embarked upon a career that soon became a journey of torment that lasted for seven long years. Wounded in self-blame,

---

[1] *A Commentary on Working Life;* Albert Camus.

I tried numerous strategies to extricate myself from this nightmare occupation but none had any lasting effect.

Then one day a mysterious voice spoke into my working world, transforming me into someone filled with hope, purpose and confidence.

God is around us all the time but we know it not until he appears.

Over time this voice became a person to me and our relationship changed my whole life.

This is the true story of my rite of passage into the world of work. I hope it will impact you with the wonderful reality of knowing genuine fulfilment in your everyday working life.

1

Without Purpose

GROWING UP IN A SECURE middle class environment in England in the second half of the twentieth century, I enjoyed primary school but not really high school. I loved sports and music but did not excel enough for them to become my livelihood. From the age of sixteen I worked as a petrol pump attendant on Saturdays, and a hotel porter and then printer's assistant during two consecutive school summer holidays. These part time jobs gave me some valuable life experiences and a bit of pocket money, but none pointed the way to my long-term career.

Consequently, I spent the last two years of high school worrying anxiously what in the world to do for a job once academic life was over. My loving, career-minded parents came up with a solution, and I promptly departed for London with my father to a Careers Guidance Bureau. The idea was that a completed questionnaire fed into a computer would spew out the perfect occupation for me. In the event, it came up with a selection of several professions. Accountancy was one of them but I remained hesitant. Yet after testing out my suitability during a school vacation at a local firm, I gave in, mainly due to the friendliness of my colleagues.

So that was the vocation I pursued – but there was a significant problem. This choice was made in the absence of my own clear ambitions. Instead it conformed to the image of those speaking into my life and profoundly disagreed with me from the very start!

2

Beginnings

AFTER COMPLETING MY secondary school education, I commenced my newly chosen career by attending a local polytechnic (now 'metropolitan university') for a nine-month foundation course. Here I studied a variety of subjects, most of which I enjoyed, apart from Accountancy which took me twice as long to pass! When this finished I started the 'job for life' in earnest as an articled clerk to a chartered accountant in my hometown. I vividly remember walking up the stone steps on my first day, opening a large blue door and crossing the threshold. It was the 2nd August, 1976, fifty days short of my twenty-first birthday.

As I stepped into the musty surroundings I was warmly greeted by a senior member of staff – the kind that has been there for half a century and quite indistinguishable from the antique furniture around them. To my surprise, he led me to my own office.

I was nervously trying to settle in behind a large, varnished oak desk wondering what to do next, when another man arrived through the door. He was the new senior auditor, Mr Blackburn. I was the new junior clerk, Mr Black, and it was I who was in the wrong place! The issue of mistaken identity was soon remedied by hastily removing me out of his way and into a much larger office full of spirited young people. My life amongst the accounting fraternity had begun.

This establishment was my work headquarters for the next two years. I was never particularly happy. I carried a deep sense of futility, often walking home with the sad reflection of having achieved nothing all day, especially when office antics were a major distraction. Having a dartboard didn't help!

I didn't really want to be there so I got up late, arriving only just in the nick of time, then suffered guilt because it was not in my nature to behave like that. I had no genuine desire to carry on part-time study towards a full Accountancy qualification, but just slogged on like a tired Sisyphus trudging back down the hill.

Visits to business premises for the official examination (auditing) of financial records proved a light relief simply because of the change of environment and people. Nevertheless, my mind was so numbed by the work that it was always drifting elsewhere.

I penned a daily journal at the time to process my thoughts.

> My intense dislike for Accountancy is always on my mind and it ruins the day. I went into the Careers Office at lunchtime, with the idea of doing a full time course in Estate Management and came away totally bewildered! Then returned to work and had to repeat something for my boss; I just

can't get on with him and don't know what he's talking about.

Tap, tap on the calculator, row upon row, line upon line of numbers, trying to make the totals balance with some schedule or other so it all made sense to someone. I wrote down my frustrations:

Didn't I struggle with maths at school? Yes, I did. So what am I doing here? Why can't I be doing something I enjoy? What do I enjoy? I don't know! ARGH!

Trying to achieve a Trial Balance felt like a courtroom trial in which I was in the dock, fighting for my life in front of a judge and jury! I blamed myself for this predicament and reasoned in my journal:

If I can be a better person, things are bound to improve.

And there were plenty of self-help books available telling me how to do just that.

One of them was 'How to Win Friends and Influence People' by Dale Carnegie, from which I discovered six rules that would revolutionise my life:

1. Become genuinely interested in other people.
2. Smile.
3. Remember that a man's name is to him the sweetest and most important sound in the English language.
4. Be a good listener. Encourage others to talk about themselves.
5. Talk in terms of the other man's interest.

6. Make the other person feel important – and do it sincerely.

To a certain extent Mr Carnegie's suggestions lifted my inner expectations, and together with a colleague I found the courage to resign from my job in favour of higher pay and better prospects elsewhere. My collaborator went away into Industry, and I to another Accountancy job in the town.

Prior to the interview for this job a curious thing happened. The man whose post I was applying for could have been my twin – bespeckled with wavy auburn hair and a beard to match. When he was showing me around the offices I struggled to concentrate on our conversation because of this peculiarity. Even his mannerisms were similar to mine!

After a very cordial interview, I was delighted to accept this new position within a few days.

So, my futile existence was seemingly remedied, but the stimulation this created was to be short-lived. My self-assurance was to hit an all-time low, and Mr Carnegie's rules were to be of no help whatsoever!

The business was positioned in a beautiful park area of the town, and my employment package very favourable regarding salary and study leave, so I was looking forward to a much happier experience of work. The early days certainly proved this to be the case and I even enjoyed a game of tennis with a colleague on a nearby court after my second week. Things couldn't be better.

However, within a month my working life had taken a dramatic nose-dive. The honeymoon period over, work became a soul-destroying nightmare, which made me yearn for my previous employment. At least there I had been able to leave the office to visit interesting environments and people.

Here I felt trapped within four walls whilst assigned the daily task of collating endless statistics for monthly cost spreadsheets, and having to scrutinise minute data on obscure microfilm by squinting at it through the murky light of the display screen.

Worse still, rather than escape at the end of the day, my evenings were a battleground of tortuous Accountancy coursework.

It was in my nature to work intensely hard, but the monotonous nature of the work caused 'paralysis' in my mind and my work rate must have slowed considerably. Sisyphus' boulder was getting heavier by the day!

My position may have been a little more bearable had there been caring support, but there was not, for my manager seemed to hate me more than I hated the work!

In some ways I can't blame her but the trouble was that it all became very personal. She had quickly grown to dislike me and I could do nothing to change her mind. My exit from the previous job had been a doorway into hell.

Looking back, I wonder if my close resemblance to my predecessor, who had obviously made a success of the job before being promoted elsewhere, had helped them in the decision to employ me. Did I have the face and demeanour of an accountant? My wife has often said, jokingly, that I did!

Well, whatever demeanour I had, it was not helping me now, and I would visit the toilet facilities regularly just to escape the merciless spiritual mood of the office. By gazing outside through a small window on tiptoes, I could just make out a beech hedge with tree covering and often this would glow under the illumination of a bright sun. I desperately yearned for this light whilst being held in by walls of darkness. Then I'd reluctantly return to my desk to try yet again to please my manager's cold heart.

I remember a pleasant young man, who worked across the office from me, who would often look over at me perplexed by this conflict situation. His anguished face read, "Why are you being treated like this?" He, like me, couldn't work out what was going on. But he couldn't help either. Neither could the kinder staff in the admin office upstairs who, despite their many years of bureaucratic service, kept their heads well down at the first signs of confrontation.

I couldn't do right for doing wrong. I once again blamed myself for it: "There must be something wrong with me!" I poured contempt on myself and even had suicidal thoughts drift in and out. I was a hopeless case! When friends asked me how my job was going, I would cover up by saying things were fine, and at the same time feeling a painful knot in my stomach.

Whilst at a Christmas party I sought the help of a retired man by asking him discretely whether, at twenty-three, it was too late to change career. His reply filled me with dread: "This is your career (for life), so stick at it." I unwillingly respected the older man's viewpoint and concluded that there was still something wrong with me!

Intensive self-analysis followed. If I wasn't up to scratch, maybe I should become like someone else. Being anyone was better than being myself because I wasn't acceptable at work, where I spent the majority of my waking hours. My manager didn't like me and neither did I.

Thus began the search to become someone else.

I thrashed it out in my journal:

> I'll be like James Bond. He's my hero; everyone loves him and he leads an exciting life. No! Stop the pretence and do your own thing.

I looked to other people's working lives, such as that of a successful London City businessman who had also struggled desperately with Accountancy study in his younger days. But he was determined to master it and put up with late nights and gross tiredness. His strong-mindedness ensured that he would succeed and make the best out of an almost impossible challenge.

More than a role model, this City Gent was an idol to me. My thoughts were, "If he can struggle and succeed, then so can I."

I strove to be like him.

I was driven to continue the self-help list. If only I could feel better about myself, this would help me endure and even succeed.

I wrote:

> Get rid of your lethargy, wake up to realities and get down to living the kind of life you want now and for the future.

I had five strategies for this:

1. Take more interest in your subject.
2. Sharpen up your wits.
3. Get up as soon as you're awake in the morning.

4. Become a stag, not a sheep.
5. Face problems with confidence knowing you're going to solve them.

What surprises me now looking back to this period is my apparent impotence. I look like a prisoner barred from a better world. Like Sisyphus' fate, there seemed to be no alternative than to carry on the best I could with contented acceptance. In reality, I was free to walk away anytime. But something stopped me. Perhaps I was captive to a cultural generation that gave me no choice beyond the career I had started.

In December God entered my diary. I wrote down a quote from a service on Christmas Day:

> When God shuts a door, he always opens another somewhere else.

The dawning of hope!

And then there was someone else who surely saved my life at this time. I had met my wife-to-be, Adrienne, the previous May through an organisation for young professionals. Somehow, through all this darkness, she saw in me something to like, even love. She and her family were a fresh source of strength to me.

Adrienne and I shared a belief in God and we spent our two-year courtship as members of a local church. This too proved crucial for me, not by making me into a better accountant, but strengthening me in the process of trying.

Whilst my domestic life was on the rise, the work situation was deteriorating considerably.

My diary reads:

The last few days have had their moments of trauma. I slave away at work only to now receive a written warning. It all seems so unfair, yet typical of this ghastly place. The natural beauty surrounding this office tries hard to give it some attractiveness of its own but it is disempowered to do so. The people within its walls won't let it.

The staff union now became involved.

I am preparing my statement. I hate recalling the past ten months. It's like giving evidence in court of a gruesome murder that I witnessed, but which I want to totally forget because it was so awful, so confusingly brutal and unjust. I am under pressure to apply for any job that comes along. But I hate preconceived ideas of jobs, and while I have time to search properly, I refuse to be pushed into a career I don't want.

By this time Adrienne and I were engaged and had booked our wedding for September, just nine months away. But with the future of my work being so unpredictable, these plans were thrown into doubt. We talked of postponing it until my job situation was safer.

A palpable tension escalated during my final weeks. Would I make it out of the door on my terms before they sacked me on theirs?

I continued with what I described as my "futile work", whilst my abrasive manager was...

...worse than ever, possessing some hard streak which just will not crack towards me. She has no pity for me whatsoever.

The Helper

A great help at this time was Andrew, our vicar. His encouraging words lifted my sunken spirit, at least for a time. His advice was to go ahead with the wedding – even if we had to live in a shed! And to apply for lots of jobs so that as many doors as possible would open.

This may have prompted me to remember the words from the Christmas Day service, now already a year ago.

Lying on my bed that night against a warm radiator, I wrote:

> I'm still a child at heart, terrified of the outside world.

A month later, at last a ray of hope began to shine into my dark world. I attended an interview for a job as Senior Auditor in a city twenty miles away. My journal describes the event:

> The interview on Friday, 1st February, 1980 went very well. So well, I was offered the job on the spot!

My interviewer was a very genial middle-aged man with a mass of white, curly hair. He was the very apparition of my Saviour!

However, a condition of accepting the job was a commitment by me to continue studying towards full qualification, and this filled me with dread!

I wrote:

> As soon as exams are mentioned I lose all confidence. Before I was happy with the job prospects; now I don't even know whether to accept it because they're keen on training and exams. When I'm confident, I tell myself that I can do it as long as I get interested enough and can

> dedicate myself to it. When I'm not confident, I'm
> a hopeless wreck and know that past failures will
> present themselves again in the future. I hope God
> and Adrienne will help me through. God knows
> I'm in a hopeless mess!

So even now, with a way out of hell, the cords of doom seemed to hold me fast. It was as though the spirits of Despair and Hope were battling for my life! Despair was lying, telling me I was no good, whilst Hope encouraged me to press on and not give up.

By the next journal entry, Hope was winning:

> God has decided for me.

During the past three weeks a serious battle had taken place. The management had started turning the screw at every possible opportunity. They wanted me to leave but when I revealed that I had attended for an interview on a day when I should have been at college, I was accused of fraud. I was doing my best to move on but my best wasn't good enough for them. It never had been! I think this was the first time I began to get angry. No longer the depressed mouse with all the problems, something rose up in me that screamed, "INJUSTICE!" Then, as if brought about by my anger, the official written job offer arrived in the post. The door had opened! I could now resign. Hope beckoned again!

This job was miraculous because my white-haired 'saviour' didn't ask for any references from my current employers. This may seem foolish but it was exactly what I needed at the time. If he had asked for a reference, my conniving management probably would have blocked my progress with an overly negative report, leaving me jobless. But, thank God, they weren't handed that opportunity.

Despair was defeated that day.

3

A New Kind of Life

ON MONDAY, 10TH MARCH, 1980 I started my new job as a senior auditor. I wrote:

> A new era is beginning. I pray to God this job will work. If I have the right people and tuition, I know the hard work will follow.

It *was* new, but not a new era in my working life. That would have to wait a while yet – but it was on its way.

I moved into temporary lodgings in the area under the care of a landlady, a retired nurse matron. Marjorie was a no-nonsense yet kind-hearted soul who was to impact my life in more ways than I then realised, starting with a comfortable bed, wholesome Yorkshire cuisine and spectacular views over the city of Bradford.

My fiancée and I were married in September, as planned, and started our life together in a village sitting snugly between the cities of Leeds and Bradford in West Yorkshire. We were living in blissful liberation. But it was not to last!

The Helper

On moving away from our hometown, we found no other church with the same strengthening warmth of spiritual life, and Sunday mornings became opportunities to sleep in.

Whilst I was settling in to a much pleasanter experience of accountancy, mainly due to the amiability of my new colleagues, Adrienne was now suffering in her place of work at a bank. She had always enjoyed her career and had been transferred to a branch in the locality of our new home. But within a few weeks it became clear that all was not well. My naturally exuberant and vivacious companion became quiet and introverted. She dreaded the thought of work and as I drove her there in the mornings, she would frequently ask me to take her back home early in the journey because of feeling unwell. Our GP would not prescribe tablets and suggested rest for stress. But rest did not help and the symptoms persisted.

As time went on it became clear that Adrienne was being systematically bullied. Tricks were played on her; she was embarrassed, mocked and insulted – all because she had come from outside the area. The management was too weak to intervene and Adrienne was becoming a shadow of her true self.

At the same time, a work colleague lent me a book on the subject of positive thinking. Within its pages was a Bible scripture from Philippians 4:13:

> I can do all things through Christ who strengthens me.
>
> (NKJV)

This became a regular declaration for Adrienne and proved immensely beneficial.

However, six months on, she could take it no more and I accompanied her to head office to sort things out. There, I was reminded of my 'saviour' from the previous year as the Human Resources Director said to Adrienne, "Right, I'll transfer you a.s.a.p." He was offering an instant way out and the relief was palpable. She never returned and was relocated to a branch in a different city where she remained content for three years before leaving to have our first child.

As for me, the auditing job provided a much kinder environment than either of my previous jobs had, but I continued to suffer profound dissatisfaction towards my work.

The best part of auditing was meeting interesting people in a diversity of business establishments. When gathering accounting information from company staff, I would frequently forget what they had told me because I was more fascinated by their personal characteristics. What made them tick? What were their likes and dislikes? What was family life like?

I was more naturally a people-auditor than a numbers-auditor!

And I dreamed of better things.

I preferred poetry writing to checking columns of figures, and my poems from that time express a desire for something more that I could not seem to grasp.

I continued the agony of dreaming through my journal:

> I live from day to day, wishing that I was better at my job. It seems my ambitions cannot be satisfied. I see people around me at work, either colleagues or clients, and how good they are at what they do. I'm no good at my job and they are! What makes them like they are? What makes me like I am? We are poles apart. They are good. I am bad.

> I make up for it by trying to be a nice guy, but sometimes this isn't enough for me. What I want more than anything now is their respect for me because I am good at my job.

> Probably this is why I keep falling back on my dream of being an author. But it's only a dream – and dreams are never fulfilled!

I was intolerably bored with studying Accountancy theory, and fought hard not to fall asleep during evening classes. I wrote:

> I am tortured by the word 'study'. Will I ever have enough incentive to get my head down? I haven't done any study for a week. It so easily slips by. I only seem to manage a couple of nights a week. I'm fighting a losing battle if I continue like this. I will just get more and more depressed by the volume of work building up. I'm losing my momentum. It's only a week since my last study and I don't know what I did.

I was also slowing down at work, taking much longer to do things than I should have.

This drove me again to self-improvement through such techniques as confident self-talk; reprimanding myself for laziness; and jogging in order to get my breathing into a good rhythm, which helped me temporarily forget my problems and calm my erratic tendencies.

The image is, once again, of Sisyphus trying and trying but not really succeeding and certainly not having any fun or fulfilment in his task.

There was a very nasty little spirit around called Not Good Enough which had been my undesirable companion for many years.

As the New Year got under way, a glimmer of hope arrived. Adrienne and I had quietly harboured a dream to have our own business one day. We would joke about having a Post Office on the Isle of Skye, and play-act imaginary business meetings in coffee shops.

Whilst our fathers had been senior employees of large corporations, we both had ancestors who were self-employed with small businesses in the ironmongery and electrical trades, and so we naturally possessed the same leaning.

So imagine our excitement, in an otherwise dull life, when a client of the auditing firm approached me with a business idea. It went like this: for a start-up cost of just £15 I could own my own business, develop it through a system of networking and one day become very rich indeed whilst doing little to earn the 'big bucks'; others would do it for me!

It was the ultimate dream. It gave us a future and a hope, and it brought us back to life!

We signed up, received our (plastic) dossier case containing all the necessary documentation and attended our first seminar. We had joined the soap-selling community.

The Helper

The seminar location exuded all the trappings of wealth, with a very grand property in a local affluent area. We were nervous on arrival, overawed by the luxury cars on the driveway where we could perhaps just make out a quiet, seductive voice whispering, "This could be yours too." And we believed that voice!

Inside we were warmly welcomed, treated to some nice coffee and tasty canapés before sitting down with just a few others to hear our speaker for the evening. Here, Adrienne and I were to learn what a motivational speaker sounds and feels like. It left us with the exuberant sensation that we could sell to the world. It was a feeling we learnt to distrust over time.

The slightly built, rather edgy middle-aged man in a plain grey suit sold us the dream for a good hour, but soon into his presentation I found myself in a world of my own, stuck on an expression he'd used: "Eating and sleeping are a waste of time!" So there I was looking at him quizzically, dwelling upon that phrase, querying, "Are you really a man who does not eat and sleep, and, if so, how on earth do you survive?' I didn't trust him!

Nevertheless, we were stimulated to action as official 'distributers', a fresh excitement to working life that put the futility of Accountancy study firmly into a rather convenient shade. We read the motivational books, declared the sales patter, "Every day we're getting better and better!" and came to lead our own seminars. We sold soap to our friends and family until their cupboards were bursting.

Once we attended a large motivational gathering, walking away convinced that the entire world wanted to buy our soap. However, by the next morning our exuberant feelings had inexplicably drained away. We learnt to call it 'hysteria'; it falsely inflated our sense of optimism.

Our distrust of this system deepened until one evening, five months on, we came to a full stop. Adrienne and I were having a drink in a local city pub, reflecting on our business, when the conversation quite surprisingly led us to the decision to quit. It was a strong mutual conviction. A 'suddenly'! We have made some excellent decisions in pubs, and this was one of them.

A year later we were to make another, and this time our lives would be changed forever!

4

From Drudgery to Freedom

THE DECISION TO DISCONTINUE soap selling may seem surprising since it was this business that had brought freshness and relief from the tedium of Accountancy, but we had made it with absolute conviction. So here it was once again, back out from the shade: a futile working life. However, as events unfolded through the last few months of 1981, a remarkable link between soap selling and a brand new career began to emerge, set in motion by an encounter in a city library.

I was sitting in the library looking out of the window, the dull view outside immensely more interesting than the Accountancy study manuals that lay before me. But in my reverie of despair, I became aware of words being spoken to me, and I listened intently:

"You are in a position to help other people."

These words are few and simple, but to me on that day a deep, deep longing was fulfilled. They held profound significance. From the very moment of hearing them, my thinking about work changed completely, as an alternative career was presented to me!

I didn't waste a minute. I was energised! It felt like I had been waiting for this moment all my life. Leaving the Accountancy manuals behind on the desk, I eagerly scoured the library shelves that day and borrowed books on careers that helped people such as social work and nursing.

Since leaving God on the doorstep of our new life together a year earlier, he had stepped back into my life, not in a religious way, but in a real, practical way to become the centre of my working life. I began to feel alive and excited about work related to this revelation, a far cry from the career in Finance that I had struggled with for so long.

Indeed I was so deeply affected by this 'calling' that conversations with God now became the overriding theme of my journal entries. I wrote in mid-December:

> It's my goal to direct people to a better way of life
> – God's way of life.

Yet this activity towards a new vocation put me in a dilemma. Now there were two careers! So how would I transition from one to the other? Despite the clear call to professional care work, I agonised desperately over it. Later in the same December entry, my diary recalls:

> I repeatedly ask God what I should do. My main worry is Accountancy study. I can start a course but cannot finish it. Only six months more and my studying will be over and yet this is just too difficult. I desperately need to think up some 'help' jobs like social work and nursing. I'm scared to say, 'No more studying,' at work. I may have to

leave. Oh God, help me make the right decision. Please!

Then a few days later I was crying out to God again:

I am not at peace with Accountancy. Please God, give me peace of mind.

Clearly, it's one thing to receive a call from God; it's quite another to put it into action smoothly and assuredly! After another few days later, I examined why people do certain jobs, the injustices in society and the merits of freedom in the education system:

I must make myself heard! In this way I can fulfil God's wishes and use what talents I have at the same time.

I had experienced a deep spiritual awakening and was suddenly full of searching questions.

My mind is full of ideas. I have an insatiable desire to know the origins of mankind; to study literature, finding the origins of the written word; comparing religions; a desperate desire to understand the world we live in, including questions about God.

My diary entries demonstrate a strength that had been absent hitherto. It was as though God, who is holy and thereby deeply interested in the downtrodden of society, was sending me into the world as one of his representatives. Yet this was only the beginning of my spiritual awakening.

The newfound confidence now led us into a scary place: the decision to quit Accountancy forever! Now back out of the shade, my futile working life was once again staring me in the face and I just couldn't carry on. I had fought to continue since there had been no alternative, but now I could end it because another vocation beckoned.

Yet it was still an agonising decision. After seven long years of exertion, was I losing all I had struggled for? Was this admitting defeat? Sometimes it's better the devil you know!

Doubts were frustrating belief.

Yet amid this turmoil, over the Christmas period, Adrienne and I came to the conclusion that I should take the risk of speaking openly and honestly with my employer about ending my Accountancy career. This decision could have left me high and dry without a job for months. It was a big gamble. But that's what I did.

On Monday, 4th January, 1982 I returned to work and set up a meeting with my senior colleagues. Their reaction was profoundly different from the unfeeling hostility of my previous employer. Indeed it ended as it had started: with the warmth of gentle kindness. They agreed that an alternative career would be a good thing and wanted to help by speaking to their own contacts in the world of professional care. One manager even suggested that I apply to enter church ministry, presumably based on some outward spiritual evidence of which I was totally unaware. Others too had recognised a change!

I'd done it. I'd stepped out and now had four months until 30th April to find the job that fitted with the call "to help other people". With financial concerns uppermost, the race was on!

Diary extracts from this time record:

> ...I have faith and know that God will now open up many avenues for my ambitions to help the ailing silent majority...

> ...I have learnt so much and yet there is so much still. The more I learn the more there is to learn. I pray to God that I shall expand my knowledge base with vigour through my faith and that this will grow stronger and stronger...

> ...By believing in God and studying the Bible I know the kind of things he wants. Therefore if I follow his 'code of ethics', I am listening to him and he is speaking to me...

The end of January came quickly. Three months to go and the deadline beckoned! Over time nursing had become the favoured option and although I could do my bit towards getting a job, I was also desperately hanging on to the vague notion that God would play his part too. After all, he'd led me into this!

I was not to be disappointed.

Having already started to research nursing as an alternative career, and with God providing support from a few around me, including Marjorie, my former matron landlady, I plunged back into the search with renewed energy and confidence.

To test out my suitability for nursing I read the professional journals for which I developed a great appetite and which excited me to 'have a go'. So I did. I signed up for two voluntary jobs: one at the local general hospital where I worked Saturday mornings on the Acute Surgical Ward; the other at a home for severely disabled people on Tuesday evenings. In time I found both very rewarding indeed.

Due to these far more attractive work experiences, my 'futile working life' was not only demoted back into the shade; it lay tiny and dormant, out of sight in a dark place pending expulsion. What a nice feeling that was!

However, during this four-month period I experienced a desperate internal battle between positives and negatives in my relationship with God.

On the positive side, I experienced a spiritual awakening. It was as though a 'Download' button had been pressed on a website, resulting in large amounts of data being received. I felt inspired to write about people-centred versus God-centred living:

> God is around us all the time. It just takes a little faith for us to open our eyes and see him working.

After an evening at the home for the disabled, I wrote:

> I can see a great interest developing for me in this area. I can see myself with the basics of life (human beings and their environment) aside from the fanciful world of money created by people (I'm in a different place looking at the world of Accountancy and Finance through new eyes). So the former is God-made and the latter man-made. The man-made things always lead to trouble, such as job pressure and domestic feuds. Money is the name of the game and self is at the heart of it. It is tragic that many good people are like this. They think it is the only way to live, but they are blind, just like those who don't know God.

> If you go after man-made things, you get caught up in the man-made world and are open to all sorts of evils.

Concerning creativity I observed:

> Creative thoughts appear in our heads. If they are not grasped immediately, you could lose them in the recesses of your mind forever. For this creativity to flourish you must be away from the real world and all its influences.

I quoted my grandfather, who gave this positive advice to his family:

> I hope they will always decide on any particular course of action not by what people may say but by whether it appears to be right or not.

Unfortunately, the negative side of the internal battle seemed to cancel out the positive thinking:

> ...I see myself amongst my possessions safe and sound. The basic man abhors me. I don't want to get my hands dirty on man. I look to the moneymaking jobs – the business professions. My thoughts have changed drastically over a month...

> I have too many ideas floating around in my head. They rise to the surface, stay for a while, and then sink back into oblivion. Some ideas are careers, some to strengthen myself. If I can capture them on paper before they sink back, I may be able to establish some pattern to my thinking. From there I hope to understand myself better and so identify an aim in life. I seem to be floating nowhere after rejecting God. I must establish some strength base and work from there...

As I lose sight of God here, I drift into do-it-yourself mode and write a list of dos and don'ts, which I have got into the practice of doing over the years; that is, giving myself a hard time. For instance:

> Toughen up, be positive, set yourself goals, make clean-cut decisions, be lively and enthusiastic, be happy and optimistic.
>
> I should have a point of view.
>
> I can't express myself.

Then:

> If you can express yourself in life you can go anywhere and do anything in the world. When you drift aimlessly it is time to plan ahead to feel secure.

That was the issue: security. Outside of God I was relying on old mind techniques to anchor my security at a time of major transition.

February flew by and still there was no sign of a job. But come the dawning of April, with just twenty-seven days to go to the deadline, I became a transformed man:

> I am happy and content, no worries at all.

In the intervening month of March, a miracle had taken place.

During our time of soap-selling, Adrienne and I had met a man one evening whilst promoting the business in our little home. Unknown to us, some seven months later he was to be my doorway into the world of professional care work. His job was Senior Nurse at an adolescent unit based in the grounds of a large psychiatric hospital ten miles from our address. That evening he had introduced himself, as the other participants had, by name and occupation, and I remembered his details.

When I contacted him, from my list of acquaintances with connections to nursing, he informed me that there were indeed job opportunities on the unit; in fact, there were two Nursing Assistant posts available. He invited me to come and look around. I did and he encouraged me to apply. So I did that too!

I attended for an interview in due course.

Career-wise, it is a big leap from number-care to people-care, and although I knew and God knew that this was the direction of flight, my interviewers were not convinced. I did not fit the criteria on that day of discussion and was turned down by phone the same evening.

I was numb. I had been so expectant. Surely this had been the much-needed miracle job. Two jobs and I couldn't even get one of them! I lamented:

> So not even God could span such a wide career
> chasm!

Then, quite unexpectedly, I received another call from the unit the following morning. They were, after all, offering me a job. One of the chosen candidates had decided against accepting and his place was mine!

I was numbed again, but this time it felt a lot, lot better. I was, as I described it, "happy and content". Everything was in place for the most radical work shift of my life to date.

My diary records probably the most positive entry I had ever written:

> I finish as an accountant on 30th April and start my nursing career on the 4th May. I have bought new clothes and am wearing them this weekend. I feel so good in new jeans and stripy tank top. Everything seems to be clicking into place and God seems nearer every day.
>
> He made the decision for me to work as a nurse and now after all the worry of changeover he is back as if saying, "I told you everything would work out." I am excited for my new career but – my God! – I hope it does work out! It's a risk. But let's face it, Accountancy was a dead-end for me. I have a new lease of life, so let's make it work.

My spiritual awakening was now cantering on apace. My diary describes a man who had come to life and was almost frantic to know all there was to know. It was an energy determined to make up for lost time.

Like a long distance runner, I was pounding down the last sixteen days before crashing through the winner's tape to an exuberant victory, and – oh, the crowds! Hebrews 11:39-12:1 describes the crowd of spiritual pioneers who have gone on ahead, and who stand cheering us on to victory. All around the stadium, they were up on their feet, arms raised, shouting and applauding; an ecstatic multitude! And I never even knew they were there!

Finally, on the 30th April my diary records:

> Today I have finished Accountancy completely. Seven years of trying to stimulate interest in a

career so dull as to narrow my mind forever. I rejoice that I can now look forward to a profession that is worthwhile and fulfilling. I should now be able to change into someone who is surer of himself, positive in outlook with no looking back. All life is to live for, so off I go! A new era is beginning.

I was learning that when God is the centre of your life, he opens doors and his timing is perfect.

From this period of my life onwards, God and work always went together. I never again wanted a job that he did not want me to have or had not prepared me for. I was sold out to him – and had every reason to be!

NOTE: The author would like to assure the Accountancy profession that he bears them no ill. Indeed he recognises their immense value to the business and working community. To those clearly suited to be accountants, he wishes them a long and enjoyable career.

5

Into the New With the Old

I STARTED MY NEW JOB as a nursing assistant on the 4th May, spending my first week in induction training, the theory of which I found very engrossing. But I carried an anxiety in the pit of my stomach in anticipation of actually meeting the unit residents at the heart of these discussions. The excitement of new things had finally worn off and I was scared to death!

> I halt at every crossroads, fearful of embarrassment, criticism and my weaknesses being exposed. Generally I have no confidence in myself.

The old baggage had come into the new era, naturally. I had known it would.

> Seven years of low confidence is hard to rectify; it will not happen overnight. It will take many months of positive thinking to straighten myself out.

My plan was simple: to "prepare and act on a programme of confidence-boosting projects". But this was just the old Andy writing motivational lists and striving to do things as if it all depended upon him, like it used to be before God had introduced Himself. The old default!

Subsequently, my first days of work on the adolescent unit were spent in fear, trying to avoid the clientele at all costs. With behaviour such as alcohol abuse, glue sniffing, school exclusion, burglary and car theft to name but a few, they were an unruly bunch of kids who could discern my fear a long way off. They were certainly not scared of me and so could take all the advantages they deemed necessary. I clung for life to the other staff who demonstrated a cool strength, which the adolescents by and large respected.

Then in my third week I was handed a breakthrough. I was 'hiding' in the secretary's office when one of the teenagers, obviously curious about me, threw his cuddly toy – a tatty, long-eared rabbit – into the room and followed it in, thereby confronting me face to face. There was no escape and only the secretary for protection, which was no protection at all!

But his manner was not threatening in the least and he began to pour out his problems to me. I just stood and listened. There was no financial information to discard in boredom; it was all about him and his life, and I loved it! All of a sudden I found myself doing what God had said: helping others.

At the same time, I too was being helped.

At the heart of the establishment's values was its identity as a "therapeutic community". The approach was not, "We're the adults, we know all and you will learn from us," but rather, "We are all in this together to learn from each other."

So God had not only brought me to a place to help, but also to be helped in being set free from some of my own baggage.

I was regularly terrified before a shift, due to the unpredictable nature of the work. The incoming staff would never quite know what awaited them, or precisely which team members would be there to support them. The unit environment could be calm or scarily volatile. It varied from day to day depending on the interpersonal dynamics of the troubled youth or staff or both. Close teamwork was a crucial ingredient to care management and personal safety.

The fear of danger was a habitual presence throughout my time there, even as I became more confident. But this growing security was based on what I'd learnt to say from others (parrot fashion) and do in given circumstances. For instance, when a young person was behaving irresponsibly, I learnt to challenge them with the phrase, "Pick up your responsibilities," and it usually had the desired effect. Beyond that learning was the 'scary unknown', and that's where God came in, for what I did not know, he did. He became the one I trusted in. He had to, for my survival!

Similar to Accountancy work, it was a job with a harsh reality to it. I didn't really want to "help others" who were scary adolescents, but I had to because I was required to. Yet this time the experience was different because I was working to my strengths (people), not striving constantly to improve my weaknesses (numbers).

Previously, I had been required to do a job in the absence of my own ambition or dreams. But this career was God's idea and he was enabling me to be whom he had created me to be and to overcome in his strength.

In the early days, prior to a shift, I couldn't leave our home unless I'd had a cup of tea. I clung to the warmth of my hot mug like a security blanket. Then I would leave for work on a wave of my wife's "You can do it!" encouragement.

Over time, God's Word superseded hot tea. Trusting that he had put me in this place was always a great reassurance, because if he had not then I was dead! Or so the fear told me.

He required me to persevere despite the dread. So as well as his spiritual presence to help, I had his encouragement from the Bible. One strengthening promise that I always declared on my journeys to work was:

> God has not given me a spirit of fear, but of power
> and of love and a sound mind.
> 2 Timothy 1:7 (NKJV)

Being aware of God in our lives is one thing; having a heart-connection with the dimension of church – Christ's body on earth – is quite another. This connection is intended to be an association or family, which helps us grow in God, but perhaps even more importantly, it exists for our spiritual protection.

Not having been related to any church since our married life had begun twenty months earlier, our position was isolated. As such we were vulnerable to enticement into supernatural spheres that would have seriously jeopardised our newfound relationship with God.

Scouring the bookshelves at work one day I came across the subject of white witchcraft. Its reading assured me that it was good since it was white and not black. As a man with little confidence or strength of character, it beguiled me by its focus on power. It was a very seductive proposition and I was left motivated to pursue it as something that appeared very good to me.

Another attraction was transcendental meditation, a fashionable accessory at the time. I saw it advertised in the same city library that had been the place of my life-changing revelation. Again, I was transfixed by its alluring promises such as peace and joy. Apparently, all I had to do was receive a mantra, then I'd be on my way to their fulfilment. I made a mental note of the date for mantra collection and returned a couple of weeks later. However, to my dismay I discovered that there was a financial cost involved. This stopped me in my tracks. I said to myself, "Why would I pay for a spiritual experience when the last one was for free? And it amazingly transformed my life. I don't need another one."

I came to my senses there and then, and that was the end of that!

6

A Spiritual Acceleration

OCTOBER ARRIVED AND GOD'S big rescue plan was upon us! This was a time when he came into both our lives in a powerfully dynamic way. We had known him and been blessed by him but what was about to happen was beyond anything we had experienced before.

My wife, Adrienne, worked at a bank in the city and was taking an unusual lunchbreak. Instead of eating in the staff room, as was the norm, she visited a shop, as recommended by a colleague, to buy some cheese for me. Whilst there she became very thirsty, bought a drink and then went and sat outside to drink it with her sandwich lunch.

All of a sudden a car pulled up near to where she was seated. Out jumped a group of young people who started performing a drama sketch. Adrienne was quite taken with it! She noticed a billboard on display reading, "Luis Palau. 7.30 tonight, Woodhouse Moor." She made a quick note in her diary and could still hear the sounds of the inspired street theatre as she headed back to keep her appointment with the afternoon shift.

Adrienne forgot about the advertised event until we met up that evening for a drink in a local pub. It was Friday, 31st October (Halloween) and we had no plans, so decided to go along. We had no idea what we were going to. Mr Palau could have been a comedian for all we knew![2] In fact, God was inviting us to a party – a heavenly one.

When we arrived, there was a giant marquee on the moor and hundreds of people queuing to get in. We joined them but when we got to the front the tent was full. Three thousand full! So we were directed to an ancient church across the road to where the 'show' was electronically linked.

We guessed it was some sort of religious event from that. Inside there was plenty of room and a large screen relaying a music band from the marquee. We sat and waited. Then just as Luis Palau was walking onto the stage, the relay hit problems, the screen went fuzzy and the poor organisers lost the feed entirely.

With red faces they suggested we sing a few hymns, after which they announced that counsel was available to help anyone interested in knowing more about Jesus. Adrienne and I turned to each another, convicted to go to this. God had touched us both at the same time, despite not hearing a word from Mr Palau! The Holy Spirit had come upon us and we were changed from the inside out.

---

[2] Luis Palau is actually an evangelist from Argentina. He can be found at *palau.org*.

It reminds us of Saul's Damascus Road experience related in the Book of Acts.[3] I had actually been experiencing the presence of the Holy Spirit several times in the preceding weeks without knowing what it was. I had sensed a warm, peaceful feeling that would come and go, though I did not want it to leave. That night the Holy Spirit came and he stayed!

Adrienne and I did not commit to anything that night due to caution, and might have drifted away once more but for a divine appointment. We had stayed so long in deep discussion, repelling the pressure to commit to Christ, that we were the last to leave. The front door being locked, we left by the back exit and as we stumbled out into the street, the darkness suddenly revealed a young student resplendent in a university scarf, a bible under his arm and a curry takeaway in his hands.

We were somewhat startled by his appearing, but more so by the fact that he was both young and a follower of Christ, for in our narrow experience we had only ever known older churchgoers!

He asked us if we had been in the church, and when we told him of our encounter, he said he would pray for us and wrote down our names in the back of his bible. He told us of a further meeting the next afternoon, which was to prove vital for our ongoing relationship with God. As he left us he seemed to vanish back into the dark of night. His name was Christian and we like to think of him as our angel.

The following afternoon we returned, grabbed a seat in the marquee near the front, heard Luis Palau speak

---

[3] See Acts 9

and went up for ministry again. We received further counsel, a copy of St John's Gospel and were connected with a family who were to help us on the next stage of our journey.

My diary records what transpired when we returned home that afternoon of Saturday, 1st November:

> Adrienne and I have made our commitment to the Lord Jesus with these words: "Oh God, I know I am a sinner. I believe Jesus Christ died for my sins. Right now, I repent and turn from my sins. I open the door to my heart and life and receive Jesus Christ as my personal Saviour. I thank you now for saving me. Amen."

It wasn't until we read the copy of St John's Gospel that same afternoon that we understood the full significance of the step we had taken. As we read chapter 3, verse 3, Jesus' words seemed to shout out to us:

> ...Very truly I tell you, no one can see the kingdom of God unless they are born again.
>
> (NIV)

Impacted by this, we realised with great excitement that we had been spiritually reborn. Life was starting afresh, and this time around we were in conscious relationship with our creator, with a spiritual home at a church in Leeds.

This prospect delighted us!

It was also to profoundly affect my working life...

7

All Change

AFTER JUST FOUR MONTHS of working with the adolescent team, a miraculous opportunity arrived for progression, which had been unobtainable before I had joined the unit, and I departed to the School of Nursing to undertake a three year course to become a qualified psychiatric nurse (RMN).

My new career had been launched and now I was being propelled into its full spectrum.

I had been released from the adolescents but this was no liberty from fearful situations. The next three years of learning with a very disparate group of students and helping people with a whole range of mental and physical disorders from ages four to ninety-four was very demanding. But God was spiritually equipping me for what I had to face, so much so that I actively chose to return to that "scarily volatile place", the adolescent unit, for two further working stints, the final period lasting over four years. It was no coincidence.

So I grew in confidence naturally in the experience of work, and spiritually in my encounters with God. The natural and the spiritual always went hand in hand, a partnership.

Church, our spiritual home, changed three times in the next ten years, each move inspired by God, thereby enhancing our relationship with him and others.

For the first time in my whole life I actually enjoyed studying! On the RMN course the theory and practice directly related to one another, a learning style that fitted me perfectly – six weeks in school followed by three months caring for patients and then back again to dissect the practical experiences, before adding more to our theory base along with interpersonal skills training. I excelled at classroom work, gaining high marks for essays, and learnt exam techniques that worked well for me.

The difference between this learning experience and the previous one in Accountancy was so great that it was like being in two completely different worlds. And spiritually I suppose I was!

I received my final exam results in the autumn of 1985. I collected the morning post and then went into the kitchen to open the envelope. With breath held I opened it and unfolded the paper.

It told me I had passed.

As I read those words a spirit of strength surged through my body and I screamed, "YES!" And that elation lasted many days and acted as a healing agent for so much struggle and past failings in both Accountancy and school before that.

I was incredibly thankful to God!

On the domestic front, Adrienne had desperately yearned for a baby two years into our marriage, but we earned insufficient income. If she gave up her banking work, we would have even less, particularly as she earned more than me on a student wage. It was an impossible dream. Or so we thought.

We remembered how three years previously my nightmare job situation had almost hindered our marriage plans. We had talked of postponing it until my job situation was safer. Yet Andrew, our vicar, had advised us to go ahead. It was a cry to persevere, despite all the obstacles. A dream remains without hope unless certain barriers are removed to bring that hope and then fulfilment of the dream. Once again we faced the battle between Despair and Hope.

So after much thought and prayer we became sure that we would rather be nearer to God than be satisfied with possessions, and we would have a baby even if it meant selling the car and moving to a cheaper house.

I found Jesus' words of Luke 12:15 helpful:

> A person's true life is not made up of the things he owns, no matter how rich he may be.
>
> (GNB)

I also recorded in my journal:

> ...The money situation will be tight, even scary at times. But our faith in the Lord will pull us through. The truth is that you can never afford to have children when material possessions are more important than people. But surely materialism cannot replace the delight of children...

> ...With my desire for people as the most important thing, child rearing and helping other people should be a lifelong career; the 'self' put away in a

box and locked. This selfless existence brings
union with God that much closer. In turn your
faith grows even stronger. There is a circle of
magical beauty. One of love, hope and faith.

Before we finally settled the issue we decided to ask
others. The response was mixed, from the worried –
"You won't be able to manage with rising costs." – to
the faith-filled – "The Lord has always provided for me.
The money always comes in when needed."

The last person we saw was our vicar, Michael. We
met with him in the evening of 20th July, 1983, on a day
when others had led me to have serious doubts about
going ahead with our baby plans. But he, a man full of
faith, said, "If I were you, I'd go ahead. No question!"
He added, "Give your worries to the Lord and he will
provide in his mysterious but marvellous way."

Michael gave us a list, but it was not a self-help list!
He advised us to use a formula for discerning the Lord's
guidance, which he called the 4 Cs:

1. (Inner) Conviction.
2. Circumstances.
3. Church (discussion with others).
4. Correctness (doors open/closed).

We lined this list up against our life and had peace
that there was an alignment.

From 1984 to 1987 Adrienne gave birth to three
beautiful daughters. We never did sell the car or move to
a cheaper house. In fact, we later moved within the
village to a larger family home, before God once again
moved us elsewhere, this time to a lovely town in North

Yorkshire. Today our daughters love God, as we do, and they relate to him closely in their own working lives.

Completing my nursing course was not the end of study for me. Far from being abhorred by it, I relished it because of my love for the subject matter. I developed a belief that I could do more than just practise my 'helping' art; I could also teach it. So I began putting together learning packages for junior staff. This led me to attend a part-time teaching course at the same metropolitan university where I had struggled with Accountancy twelve years earlier. This time I was a new man with a new subject; I graduated three years after qualifying as a nurse.

Then five years later I moved out of nursing practice altogether and into full time teaching at a college of further education as a Social Care lecturer, with yet more university academic study towards higher teaching qualifications.

And that was not all.

Prior to leaving the nursing profession in 1993, I studied for a counselling qualification followed by another two years from 1996 to 1998.

This enabled me to pursue yet another career, as a counsellor at the college, and by the end of the decade, I was in the process of concluding my fourth career.

There would still be ups and downs in the years to come – new challenges and new lessons to be learned. But the foundations were now in place.

Epilogue

HAVING STARTED WORKING LIFE reflecting a distorted image (without a vision or ambition); becoming a churchgoer with my hero, Adrienne; to having two powerful divine experiences a year apart, one a revelation and the other a restoration; I was like a spacecraft whose flight path had been critically altered towards a new spiritual destination. The control centre back on earth was under new management and the old rulebook had been thrown out! My whole mind-set had changed. New destiny and fresh liaisons awaited me.

My diary entries reflected this dramatic change: no more the self-analysis with lists of goals to achieve, but a colourful variety of spiritually inspired writings, from sermon notes to poems, family experiences to conversations with God on a whole range of subjects. Creative joy replaced desperate striving. Some personal issues still needed sifting through, but strength slowly but surely replaced impotence.

I had come a long, long way since Christmas 1979 when the retired man had said to me, "Accountancy is your career for life." Putting my life into God's hands has been a wonderful adventure – and it never ends.

He is the Supreme Helper.

See John 14:16
in the English Standard Version of the Bible.

About 'Work with God'

The events of this book happened many years ago and much has happened between God and the author since then.

Today Andy runs a ministry called 'Work with God', established in 2000, in which he supports, encourages and equips people who have a special calling on their life to partner with God in the work they do.

Further information can be obtained from:

www.workwithgod.co.uk

The Helper: Workbook

An Invitation

Now that you have read *The Helper,* the author would like to invite you to journey on with him in a devotional study so that your own working life may be enhanced.

This workbook is a reflection of Andy's personal journey with God in the form of thought-provoking exercises directly related to each chapter of the book. This is then followed by further chapters about the biblical origins of work with several important keys on how to partner with God in the work you do.

The Helper Workbook
Andy Black
ISBN 978-1-911086-05-5

"A spiritual adventure of enlightenment with our helper, the Holy Spirit, as guide."

The Helper: Workbook

Get your copy now from Amazon or your local bookshop, or purchase directly from the publisher:

www.onwardsandupwards.org

Publisher's Recommendations

The Christian Guide to Jobs and Careers

Charles Humphreys
ISBN 9781907509087

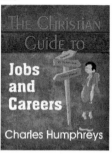

Encouragement and fresh insight into what the Bible has to say about the whole area of careers guidance. Useful for self-reflection, 1:1 support, and group work – for those who are unemployed as well as those looking for a new career direction.

Get Up, Create, Break Out

Veronica Anthony
ISBN 9781907509827

Veronica Anthony shares her knowledge and experience of supporting women to re-launch their careers. She takes us on her own personal journey of re-launching her career in the face of challenges, without compromising on her primary role as a mother. Through reflective questions and injections from stories of other women, she shows you how you can draw strength from your faith in God to overcome daily struggles and create the tools you need to break out into the marketplace.

Books available from **www.onwardsandupwards.org**